# GIFFORD PINCHOT

# GIFFORD PINCHOT

*American Forester*

by
**Peter Anderson**

A First Book
Franklin Watts
A Division of Grolier Publishing
New York / London / Hong Kong / Sydney
Danbury, Connecticut

Cover photographs copyright ©: North Wind Picture Archives; UPI/Bettmann (portrait)

Photographs copyright ©: UPI/Bettmann: pp. 2, 42, 52, 53, 54, 59; USDA Forest Service, Grey Towers: pp. 8, 9, 12; Jay Mallin/Library of Congress: pp. 14, 34, 35; North Wind Picture Archives: pp. 16, 19, 37; Special Collections Library, Duke University: pp. 21, 55; Biltmore Estate, Asheville, N.C.: pp. 25, 27, 29; Forest History Society, Durham, N.C.: p. 32 (K.D. Swan/USFS), 49; Library of Congress: p. 40; Pennsylvania State Archive, Richard J. Beamish Papers: p. 45; The Bettmann Archive: pp. 48, 58.

921
P649

Library of Congress Cataloging-in-Publication Data

Anderson, Peter, 1956–
Gifford Pinchot : American forester / by Peter Anderson.
p. cm. — (A First book)
Includes bibliographical references (p. ) and index.
ISBN 0-531-20205-4
1. Pinchot, Gifford, 1865–1946—Juvenile literature.
2. Foresters—United States—Biography—Juvenile literature.
3. Conservationists—United States—Biography—Juvenile literature.
[1. Pinchot, Gifford, 1865–1946. 2. Foresters.
3. Conservationists.] I. Title. II. Series.
SD129.P5A54 1995
634.9'092—dc20
[B]                                              95-2041 CIP AC

Copyright © 1995 Peter Anderson
All rights reserved
Printed in the United States of America
6 5 4 3 2 1

# CONTENTS

29,801

CHAPTER ONE

# AT HOME IN THE WOODS

*Whatever forestry might be,*
*I was for it.*

—Gifford Pinchot

The Pinchot estate, a sprawling stone mansion surrounded by manicured lawns and rose beds, stood high on a hillside overlooking the Delaware River valley. Thick groves of oak, birch, hemlock, and maple cloaked the rolling hills. Tucked away in their shadows were waterfalls that tumbled over moss-covered boulders. Brooks ran cool and clear into deep pools where Gifford Pinchot and his younger brother, Amos, loved to fish and swim.

Young Gifford Pinchot

Trails had been cut through the trees, but Gifford preferred to blaze his own path. He sought out the deepest and darkest groves, especially in the summer when the Pennsylvania hill country got hot and muggy. For Gifford Pinchot, the woods offered an escape from the responsibilities of greeting guests at the many gatherings hosted by his parents. Better to swim and fish than dress up in a starchy, white suit. Besides, there was so much more to do in the woods. Gifford loved to collect bugs and beetles. One winter, he took the time to learn the different species of birds. In the spring, he identified all the wildflowers. A walk in the woods was like a scavenger hunt. The challenge was to see how many different insects or flowers or trees he could find in a day.

Gifford's father, James Pinchot, encouraged Gifford's love of forests and the outdoors.

James Pinchot couldn't help but notice his eldest son's love of the woods. He, too, admired the great forests of the Pennsylvania hill country, but he was worried about them. Too many trees were being cut down.

Gifford's father was among the first Americans to express concerns about dwindling forests. In Europe, where wood was less plentiful, he had seen forestry put into practice. There, timber harvests were carefully planned. Only certain trees were cut. Others were left so that the forest could renew itself.

In the United States, a country so vast that it was hard to imagine an end to the forests, many people thought that the best way to harvest timber was to cut the best and destroy the rest. Forestry practices were unheard of. If a tree wasn't worth cutting for lumber, then it might as well be cleared for farmland. For another generation of Americans to enjoy the resources of these eastern forests, that approach would have to change. At least that's what James Pinchot was thinking in the summer of 1885.

"How would you like to be a forester?" he asked his son one day that summer.

Gifford wasn't sure what a forester actually did. The only thing he knew for certain was that foresters spent a lot of time in the woods. For now that was all he needed to know.

# CHAPTER TWO

# A FORESTER'S EDUCATION

*The fact that forestry was new and strange and promised action probably had as much to do with my final choice of it as my love for the woods. . . . Action was what I craved.*

— Gifford Pinchot

When he arrived on the campus of Yale University in the fall of 1885, Gifford Pinchot found plenty of action. Out on the grassy vistas, underneath the gold-tinted leaves of the oaks and maples, Gifford was introduced to the adventures of college life. Along with his fellow freshmen, he tried to outrun

Gifford Pinchot as a student at Yale University

the upper-classmen who liked to initiate newcomers by dunking them in a fountain.

Having his room raided, his shirts and suits knotted up, and all his shoes tied together into a great snarl of laces, was all part of the initiation experience for Gifford and the other freshmen. Always respectful of the older students who pulled these pranks, Gifford accepted his fate with good humor. Later, as a long-legged running back dashing past herds of linemen, he would earn their respect on the football field.

By the time the elm trees budded out during the spring of his senior year, Gifford had earned the admiration of classmates and teachers alike. He had captained the Yale football team and established his reputation as a scholar. Courses in botany, geology, and biology had been good preparation for a forestry career. Mentors such as Dr. William Brewer, a professor of agriculture and an expert on America's woodlands, had encouraged him to pursue his dream of becoming a forester.

There were others, however, who had advised against such a choice. On a trip to Washington, D.C., in the winter at the start of 1889, Gifford talked with Bernard Fernow, a German forester employed by the U.S. government. Fernow was discouraged. Even in the government, he complained, only a few people were convinced that forest managment was important. He counseled Gifford to choose a career in botany or landscape gardening instead.

Only a few weeks before graduation, Gifford's grandfather also tried to persuade Gifford to drop the idea of a forestry career. His grandfather believed that it was Gifford's duty instead to make money by taking over the family business.

Had it not been for his family's wealth, Gifford wouldn't have been educated at America's finest

Dr. Bernhard Fernow, an early
leader of forestry in the United States

schools. Nevertheless, he saw no reason to devote his life to making more money. His family didn't need any more than it already had. Besides, wasn't serving his country more important than making money? And hadn't his father suggested forestry as a way to do that?

Once again, James Pinchot counseled his son to stick with his path. Bolstered by his father's support,

Gifford made a passionate speech on forestry during the graduation ceremonies at Yale that spring. But passion could never satisfy his need for practical experience.

"I had chosen forestry," he later wrote, "but still I did not know exactly what it was I had chosen." Book learning wasn't enough. To get the practical experience he needed, he would have to travel to Europe where forestry was practiced.

Shortly after graduation, Gifford left for England and France with his father's blessing and several letters of introduction. There he would meet professional foresters, one of whom suggested he attend a school in France.

In November 1889, Gifford took his advice and enrolled in a French forestry school. Fortunately, he had learned to speak French fluently on previous European travels. He quickly made friends with Joseph Hulot, one of his fellow forestry students.

Together, Gifford and Joseph tramped through nearby forests. There they met woodchoppers. They met peasants who carried away tiny scraps of wood that others had left behind. They met the forest guards who enforced regulations on the number and size of the trees to be cut. Wood was so valuable that even a twig the size of a pencil could be sold. Without foresters to make the rules and forest guards to enforce them, there wouldn't have been a tree in sight.

In France, Gifford learned everything he could about harvesting trees. The experience deepened his appreciation of a forest's value.

Finally, Gifford was getting the firsthand experience he needed. Silvaculture classes taught him how to grow and harvest trees efficiently. On field trips, he measured and selected trees to be cut and then he marked them accordingly. Best of all, he mastered the tools of the woodsman's trade. Gifford loved to work with an ax and a saw.

Having completed his schooling in France, Gifford apprenticed with a Swiss forester named Meister. Alongside his mentor, he worked on a forest that had been carefully managed since the time of Christopher Columbus. Meister was more than a good forester, he was a savvy politician and a community leader. Without gaining the respect of the community, Gifford realized, a forester couldn't convince others to cooperate with rules and regulations.

Under Meister's guidance, Gifford further developed the skills he needed to enter his chosen profession. There was only one problem. Back home in America, his profession was virtually unheard of. How would he be able to put these newly acquired skills to work?

# EXPLORING AMERICA'S FORESTS

# CHAPTER THREE

A friend had once asked Gifford Pinchot what he planned to do after graduating from Yale. "I am going to be a forester," said Gifford.

"What's that?" asked the friend.

"That's why I am going to be a forester," Gifford replied.

When Gifford Pinchot came home from France in 1891, few Americans knew any more about forestry than his friend at Yale had. One well-meaning woman mistook Gifford for a gardener. "A forester! How very nice!" she exclaimed after he mentioned his profession. "Perhaps you can tell me what I ought to do about my roses."

If forestry had a future in the United States, education was the key. Yet even with all his European schooling, Gifford considered himself only half-trained. He had seen forestry in action, but

SAWING INTO LOGS.

Gifford learned new logging techniques
from lumberjacks in western forests.

knew very little about American trees. If he was to promote forestry in America, he would have to see its forests first.

When Bernhard Fernow, head of the Forestry Division of the U.S. Department of Agriculture, invited him to join a forest survey in eastern Arkansas, Gifford jumped at the chance. Never before had he traveled west of Pennsylvania. He took careful notes as they rode horses through the thick groves of oak that grew along the Mississippi River. He spoke with lumberjacks who taught him new logging and sawing techniques. And he made an unlikely new friend named Betsy.

Gifford charmed Betsy right away. Letters home suggested that they were getting closer all the time. When the Pinchots began to wonder about Gifford's backwoods acquaintance, he finally revealed her true identity. Betsy was a pet bear belonging to a family in Arkansas with whom Gifford had stayed. He had befriended her with a bottle of molasses.

Gifford's adventures in Arkansas marked the beginning of his American odyssey. In 1891, he set out for Arizona to report on a company's timber holdings there. On the way, he crossed the wide rolling plains west of the Mississippi. Homesteader's cabins seemed so tiny in that vast, open land.

Gifford Pinchot married Cornelia Bryce on
August 14, 1914. Here, Gifford enjoys a day
in the country with his family.

When Gifford arrived in Bisbee, Arizona, he was met by a young cowboy who gave him a horse, a buckboard, and directions to the ranch where he had arranged to meet his guide. Gifford hadn't planned on a solo trip across the desert. Warnings of outlaws and hostile Apaches on the outskirts of town added to his uneasiness.

Nevertheless, he loaded up his gear and rode out to the edge of town where he changed out of his fancy eastern clothes. No need to attract any attention, he figured. He hid his money, loaded his gun, and set out on the trail.

Gifford hadn't gone far when he spotted four horsemen riding single file, rifles slung across their saddles. He tugged on the reins and reached for his gun, but the four men just kept on riding and disappeared behind a distant butte. What a relief it was when the adobe ranch buildings finally came into view later that day.

The cowboy guides who rode into the nearby Huachuca Mountains with Gifford the next day were impressed with his hardiness. This Pinchot character was different than the eastern city slicker they had expected. Not only could he handle an ax, but he was a deadeye shot with his rifle. Most dudes would have been complaining about saddle sores after so much riding . . . not Pinchot.

The rougher the country, the more he seemed to like it.

Gifford appreciated these wildlands and loved sleeping out under the stars. He admired the hardy pines that grew in this harsh desert country. He measured them, and cataloged them, and estimated how much lumber they might produce if they were managed well.

Once his work was done, he would continue his travels—north to the Grand Canyon and west to southern California where he would see thick groves of eucalyptus trees and giant sequoias. Further north, he would visit the great stands of Douglas fir in Oregon and Washington.

"In my first six months at home," he later wrote, "I had seen something of the forest in thirty-one states and Canada, even if only from the train, and had actually been in the woods in nine of them. Not such a bad start, although my apprenticeship was far from ended."

# PUTTING FORESTRY TO WORK

# CHAPTER FOUR

*Here was my chance . . . to prove what America did not yet understand . . . trees could be cut and the forest preserved at one and the same time. I was eager, confident, and happy as a clam at high tide.*

— Gifford Pinchot

George W. Vanderbilt's estate covered 7,000 acres (2,800 hectares) of rolling hills and bottom lands on both sides of the French Broad River in North Carolina. Biltmore, as his property was called, had once been a patchwork of small farms. Because of poor soils, these farms had never been successful. Vanderbilt hoped, with Gifford Pinchot's help, to show that these lands were better suited for growing timber.

When Gifford accepted the job of managing Biltmore's forests in December 1891, he took on an enormous challenge. It wasn't just the condition of the forest that had been slashed, burned, and over-grazed, although that was certainly challenge enough. Biltmore would be the first American wood-

The Vanderbilt mansion under construction amid acres of hills and forests

land to be managed by a forester. It was up to Gifford to prove that forestry worked. It was up to him to show that he could harvest timber, make some money, and create a healthier forest in the process.

The first step was to get out on the land. From dawn till dusk, Gifford walked through the woods carefully recording the number and variety of the trees he found. Only those trees that he notched with an ax would be logged. Everything else was to be left standing.

At first, Vanderbilt's loggers were suspicious of Gifford's approach to harvesting timber. If fewer trees were cut, wouldn't that mean fewer jobs? Gifford told of forests in Europe that had provided communities with timber and jobs for hundreds of years. Too many old trees could choke out new growth. On the other hand, old trees were needed to seed the next generation. By cutting selectively, he explained, a forester could keep the right mixture of old and young trees. This would help the forest stay healthy and sustain itself, as well as the logging profession, for future generations.

Gifford advised the loggers to clean up scraps after cutting so there would be less fuel left for forest fires. He explained techniques for cutting trees so that the trunks would not be damaged and surrounding trees would not be injured. Maybe Mr. Pinchot would like to demonstrate, suggested one of the loggers, figuring Gifford to be more of a thinker than a woodsman.

Gifford (far left) and a survey crew visit with George Vanderbilt (second from right) and friends.

Gifford grabbed an ax and cut into a tall oak. Wood chips flew through the air. It looked like this Pinchot character had handled an ax before. Finally, the old oak creaked and wavered and fell through a gap in the surrounding trees. It landed just where Gifford had intended it to.

Gifford's previous experience may have prepared him for working with Vanderbilt's logging crews, but nothing could have prepared him for his first night alone in the woods. Sleeping under the stars was nothing new. Still, in all his travels, he had always camped in the company of others. Camping alone in the Carolina forests was different.

"When you are alone in the woods at night all sounds are magnified," Gifford later wrote. "In the stillness you can hear a little noise a long way off. Small creatures move. The trees creak. . . . Dry leaves rustle."

"In the middle of the night a sound dragged me awake. . . . My fire was almost out. Thud! Thud! Something was coming! My heart was in my throat. For the only time in my life the hair was rising on my head in pure fright. . . . Whatever made those steps was coming—coming nearer and nearer!"

Whatever it was had some size to it. He could tell that by the sound of large sticks under its feet. He could hear its breathing—too late to run. A huge

George Washington Vanderbilt came from a wealthy family that was famous for donating great sums of money to charities. He devoted much of his life and wealth to the cause of conservation.

brown head poked out of the shadows. "Get outta here!" Gifford hollered, and that cow galloped off like a racehorse.

Fortunately, Gifford's first year as a working forester went better than his first night alone in the woods. After the first twelve months of work at Biltmore, he reported that the timber harvest had made money for the first time. More important, he had cut mostly old and diseased trees. Now, the Biltmore forest was healthier.

After a year of long days in the woods marking trees and long nights at a desk figuring out costs and profits, Gifford had made his case for forestry. His efforts paid off even more in 1893 when George Vanderbilt arranged to set up an exhibit of the Biltmore forestry project at the Chicago World's Fair. There, thousands of Americans would hear about forestry for the first time.

# CHAPTER FIVE

# PRIVATE FORESTS
# AND
# PUBLIC
# LANDS

*I could not escape a deep concern over the theft and destruction of the public . . . timberlands. To deal with such questions, I felt sure, would become part of my job as a forester, since Uncle Sam was . . . the greatest timberland owner of them all.*

—Gifford Pinchot

Building on the reputation he had earned at Biltmore and the Chicago World's Fair, Gifford Pinchot decided to set up his own forestry business. He compiled a list of wealthy eastern landowners who might benefit from his services as George Vanderbilt had. Then he sent them letters offering

Heavy logging on steep hillsides, as in this picture,
can leave the ground vulnerable to soil erosion.

suggestions for better management of their forests.
He hoped his efforts would pay for the office he had
opened up in New York City, and it wasn't long
before they did. Many long days of fieldwork in the
eastern forests would follow.

Success as a private forester, however, would never be enough for Gifford. Memories of his travels through the great western forests haunted him. Just as he had experienced the magnificence of these forests, he had also witnessed their abuse and destruction. Greed and the reckless harvesting of timber were only part of the problem. He had seen forestlands that had been badly eroded because of overgrazing and hillside clear-cuts. He had seen huge patches of forest that had been consumed by fire. These forests, many of them on public lands, were in desperate need of supervision and management.

To try and improve the situation, Gifford helped create a commission to examine the nation's forests and recommend management strategies to the president. At the age of thirty-one, Gifford was the youngest member of the forestry commission that included some of America's most accomplished scientists and professors. He was also the most active when it came to doing fieldwork in the western forests.

Along with several companions, he rode along the Continental Divide in Montana surveying forests, identifying tree species, and studying insect and fire damage. He took hundreds of photographs to document what he saw. Around the campfire each night, he filled notebook after notebook with his

FRANCIS WALSH INTERMEDIATE SCHOOL
29,801        LIBRARY

Gifford Pinchot camps out during a forestry survey.

observations. Somehow he found time to hunt, keeping his party well supplied with meat.

Finally, after the commission had completed surveys like this throughout the country, it was time to make recommendations to the president, Grover Cleveland. Not all of the commission members agreed on the best way to manage America's forests.

Charles Sargent headed up the presidential commission on forestry. The commission recommended to President Grover Cleveland that more forest reserves be established.

Charles Sargent, a botany professor from Harvard, believed that timber cutting should be forbidden in the forest reserves. He suggested they be patrolled by the army.

Gifford disagreed. The forest reserves, he argued, should be protected, but they should also be able to produce timber. Instead of the army patrolling the reserves, a corps of forestry rangers should manage the nation's woodlands.

As head of the commission, Sargent won out and Gifford reluctantly agreed to go along with his plan. Despite their arguments, commission members were unanimous on one point: the nation needed to set aside more forest reserves. President Cleveland agreed. At the commission's suggestion, he established thirteen new forest reserves in South Dakota, Wyoming, Montana, Idaho, Washington, Utah, and California.

While many conservationists were pleased with Cleveland's decision, western loggers, miners, and ranchers were horrified. As Charles Sargent had suggested, all reserves would be off limits to mining, woodcutting, and grazing. Western senators, none of whom the president had consulted on this issue, were bitterly opposed to any restriction on economic growth in their states. They fought the president's action and succeeded in postponing the creation of the new forest reserves.

Although fires may damage scenery temporarily, they can eventually lead to new growth and a healthier forest.

Gifford understood some of the westerners' gripes. He blamed opposition to the reserves on Sargent's plan to close them off to any kind of use. For the forest reserve system to succeed, western support was needed. The secretary of the interior sent Gifford out west to see if he could gather more evidence to support the cause.

During that summer of 1897, Gifford traveled through the western forests once again. He took photos of stripped hillsides where eroded soils clogged nearby streams. He documented the charred remains of forests decimated by fire. He collected the statements of Californians who objected to the greedy plunder of their redwood and sequoia trees. And any time he had the chance, he offered this information to newspaper reporters.

The stories they wrote not only advanced the cause of forestry, they also enhanced the reputation Gifford had already made for himself as a member of the forestry commission. Shortly after Gifford had completed his report, he was offered a new job.

The head of the government Forestry Division had resigned and a replacement was needed. No one was more qualified for the job than Gifford, at least that's what those who offered him the job had decided. Certainly no one was more eager to serve the country and defend its forests.

CHAPTER SIX

# CHIEF FORESTER

*We were all young, . . . all eager, all proud of the Division, and all fiercely determined that its attack on forest devastation must win. . . . With such a cause and such a spirit, we couldn't lose.*
—Gifford Pinchot

On his first day as chief forester in the summer of 1898, Gifford Pinchot looked around his tiny office in the attic of an old brick building in Washington, D.C. There wasn't a forestry tool in sight, not even a hatchet for marking trees. It was clear that his predecessor had spent most of his time behind a desk. If Gifford had his way, that would soon change.

A newspaper cartoon depicting
Gifford Pinchot as the nation's chief forester.

Prior to 1898, the Division of Forestry had been an obscure government office with very little influence. Even U.S. forest reserves were managed by a different government agency called the General Land Office. Gifford was determined to change that. If he had his way, U.S. forests would someday be managed by foresters, not government bureaucrats.

Until that time, the Division of Forestry could best serve the public by educating them, only Gifford's brand of education would take place in the woods, not the lecture halls. To that end, Gifford and his team made it known through newspapers across America, that the Division was ready to help lumbermen and farmers make the most of their timberlands.

Had it not been for the leadership skills Gifford had once demonstrated as captain of the Yale football team, the public's response might have overwhelmed the handful of foresters who made up his staff. Instead they followed his example and worked tirelessly. By year's end, they had inspected and made recommendations on more than 400,000 acres (160,000 hectares) of private woodlands.

To keep up such a pace, the Division would need to get more foresters out in the field and it would have to be done on a shoestring budget. Gifford

As head of the U.S. government's Division of Forestry,
Gifford Pinchot was in charge of the many young
foresters who watched over the nation's woodlands.

decided to enlist the help of young men interested in learning about forestry. He put the word out at several universities and hired his first crop of young rangers — "Pinchot's Young Men," as they came to be known — in the summer of 1899.

Here was a way, not only to carry out needed studies on America's forests, but also to train the foresters of the future. At evening gatherings at his Washington, D.C., home, Gifford treated his new recruits to gingerbread and roasted apples and inspired them with speeches on the challenges of forestry.

Like an oak from an acorn, the Division of Forestry began to take shape under Gifford's supervision. But along with the Division's growth came a mounting workload that all but buried Gifford in his tiny office at the Agriculture Building. When he was asked by the secretary of the interior to settle a dispute on a forest reserve in Arizona, he happily accepted the challenge.

Gifford arrived in Winslow, Arizona, with botanist Fred Colville. Together they would ride off to the high mesas of northern Arizona with Albert Potter, a sheep rancher, and E. C. Bunch, who represented water users in the lower valleys.

Those who irrigated in the lower valleys claimed the sheepmen had overgrazed the high mesas where the water came from. The soil, usually held in place by grasses and young trees, had eroded and clogged up reservoirs and ditches. As a result, the irrigators in the valleys had not received their water. The sheep ranchers who grazed the mesa denied any responsibility.

It was up to Pinchot and Colville to examine the evidence and settle the dispute. Off they rode under the high desert sun, their lips parched by hot, dusty winds and their shirts drenched with sweat. It seemed as though sheep rancher Albert Potter, also their guide, was trying to wear them out before they even got to the high mesa.

After several hard days in the saddle, their canteens and water bags had run dry. That night, the only available water came from a storage tank that contained the remains of a cow carcass. Gifford figured this was yet another test, so he played right along with Potter's game. He strained the water through a dishtowel and brewed up some strong tea, almost strong enough to hide the water's putrid taste. Somehow they made it through the night without getting sick.

Finally, the next day they rode up onto the high mesas and found water on the timber-covered slopes. Gifford showed Potter where the sheep had trampled young trees. Colville pointed out bare soils churned up by sheep hooves.

Gifford Pinchot loved nothing more
than to ride on horseback through a forest—
in his youth and in his old age.

Not only were these two tenderfeet surprisingly tough, Potter realized, they also knew their stuff. He couldn't deny their evidence. Later Potter would join Pinchot in his efforts to promote further grazing reforms. For now it was enough for Gifford to have solved this particular grazing feud. He had hoped to enhance his young agency's reputation by solving the conflict, and he had done just that.

# CHAPTER SEVEN

# PARTNERS WITH THE PRESIDENT

When Gifford Pinchot and Teddy Roosevelt first met, they really "hit it off." It all began with a wrestling match. Roosevelt, a lover of vigorous physical activity, challenged Pinchot to wrestle. Gifford accepted and was promptly pinned by the burly New York governor. Pinchot found revenge in the boxing match that followed. As he described it later, he "had the honor of knocking the future President of the United States off his very solid pins."

When Teddy Roosevelt became president in 1901, Gifford Pinchot became one of his most trusted advisers. Not only had Gifford won Roosevelt's respect in

Gifford Pinchot (right) with
President Theodore Roosevelt (left)

Members of this early-1900s field trip to Yosemite National Park, pictured here at the base of a giant sequoia, included Gifford Pinchot (third from right), Teddy Roosevelt (third from left), and John Muir (fourth from right). Muir, one of America's most influential wildlands advocates, helped establish Yosemite and other national parks.

the boxing ring, he had also impressed his future colleague with his knowledge and passion for forestry.

Like Gifford, Teddy Roosevelt grew up in a wealthy eastern family. Like Gifford, he had developed a passion for being outdoors. He was an avid hunter and part-time rancher who had come to know and love the forests and mountains of the East and West. It was hard for Gifford to imagine a better partner in the fight to save American forests.

Together, they would enact many of the reforms that Gifford had envisioned for the U.S. forest reserves. In 1905, thanks in part to Gifford's persistence and the president's support, Gifford's Division of Forestry finally took over the management responsibilities for these public forests. He renamed his agency the U.S. Forest Service to emphasize his intention to serve the forests and those who used them.

Gifford demanded the utmost in dedication from the first generation of rangers he sent out in the field to oversee America's forests. For a relatively low wage, a ranger was expected to work hard under the roughest conditions in isolated places. Building cabins and trails; estimating, scaling, and harvesting timber; surveying and making simple maps; fire fighting; packing and shoeing horses — these were some of the skills required of Pinchot's rangers.

Perhaps the hardest part of a ranger's job was dealing with the public. In many cases, forest users had never had to contend with anyone trying to enforce the government's rules. There were those who resented Pinchot and his corps of young foresters telling them what they could and couldn't do. In these situations, a ranger often had to play the role of a sheriff and enforce the law.

A strong contingent of Westerners opposed the government's role in managing public lands that Westerners had come to consider their own. These dissenters were especially opposed to Roosevelt's and Pinchot's desires to create new forest reserves. In 1907, Senator Fulton attached an amendment to an agriculture bill that would limit the president's power to set aside more forest reserves.

President Roosevelt had planned to sign the agriculture bill. It was a high priority. Now, if he signed it, he would have to give up his power to create new forests. With less than a week to go before the deadline for signing the bill, the president was in a fix until Gifford Pinchot came up with a plan to solve the president's dilemma.

Why not create the new forest reserves and then sign the bill?

Let them have their amendment, Gifford suggested, we can get the reserves we want, too.

The president was enthusiastic, yet perplexed. Did Pinchot really think he could gather up all the information and maps and lay out all the boundaries for the new reserves in less than a week's time?

With little time to waste, Pinchot raced back to his office.

Telegraph wires hummed with messages sent out to every forest supervisor across the country.

Among the many duties of a forester were: building bridges over streams and rivers;

watching for signs of fire;

and even building birdhouses
to help preserve the forest's bird population.

From his office in Washington, D.C., Gifford Pinchot
coordinated his vast forestry department that stretched
thousands of miles across the United States.

Pinchot had always demanded a lot of his foresters but never with this kind of urgency. Now he told them to send specifications and boundaries for as many new forests as possible. He would need them within a week.

Rangers rode out on horseback to survey boundaries for the new reserves. Supervisors compiled their notes and rushed their plans back to Forest Service headquarters in Washington. Typewriters clickety-clacked day and night as government clerks printed up the proclamations for each new forest reserve.

Pinchot ran back and forth from the White House carrying armloads of maps and documents. He and Roosevelt spread out maps on the floor. Crawling around on hands and knees they double-checked all the reserve boundaries. By midnight of their March 3 deadline, the deed was done. The new forest reserves were official.

With a great sigh of relief, Roosevelt signed the agriculture bill with only minutes to spare. Thanks to Pinchot and his corps of dedicated rangers, Roosevelt was able to put his power to work, one last time. Their last minute effort to protect some of the West's finest timberlands would be remembered as one of the great victories for the cause of conservation in America.

**CHAPTER EIGHT**

# A CONSERVA- TIONIST'S LEGACY

*The care of the forests is the duty of the nation.*

— Gifford Pinchot

In 1946, speaking on the fortieth anniversary of the U.S. Forest Service that he had helped create, an eighty-one-year-old Gifford Pinchot had this to say about his life: "I have been a governor every now and then, but I am a forester all the time—have been, and shall be, to my dying day."

After leaving office as America's chief forester, Gifford would go on to distinguish himself as a politician, serving several terms as the governor of

Gifford Pinchot as governor of Pennsylvania

Governor Pinchot and son

Pennsylvania. But forestry would forever be his first love. Only a few days before his death in October 1946, he was hard at work revising a plan for the forests on the Pinchot family estate in Pennsylvania.

He especially enjoyed his visits to the forests where he had worked as a younger man. On one such visit at the age of seventy-two, he planned to tour the forests of Montana, Idaho, Oregon, and California with two of his oldest Forest Service friends.

Prior to their departure, he announced his intention to spend a few nights under the stars. "I am going to . . . bring a small sleeping bag along with the hope that I can get a few nights in the open . . . just for the sake of old times. Gosh it's going to be great," he gleefully told his friends.

More than any one man of his generation, Gifford had helped to conserve America's forests. Now, as he toured the western forests again, Gifford met rangers carrying on the Pinchot tradition, but the forests themselves were his greatest legacy. Now, after several decades of good forest management, he felt certain that his children and their children would have these forests to enjoy. To leave them this gift brought him joy. "What else could a man ask for?", Gifford wondered as he walked through the tall pines.

# FOR FURTHER
# READING

Amdur, Richard. *Wilderness Preservation*. New York: Chelsea House Publishers, 1993.

Challand, Helen J. *Vanishing Forests*. Chicago: Children's Press, 1991.

DeStefano, Susan. *Theodore Roosevelt: Conservation President*. New York : Twenty-First Century Books, 1993.

Faber, Doris. *Nature and the Environment*. New York: Scribner, 1991.

Keene, Ann T. Earthkeepers: *Observers and Protectors of Nature*. New York: Oxford University Press, 1994.

Hirsch, S. Carl. *Guardians of Tomorrow: Pioneers in Ecology*. New York: Viking Press, 1971.

# INDEX

# ABOUT THE AUTHOR

Peter Anderson has worked as a river guide, carpenter, newspaper reporter, writing teacher, editor, and wilderness ranger. He has written ten books for young readers on topics related to nature, Native Americans, and the history of the American West. Currently, he lives in Salt Lake City, Utah.